DATE DUE

GAYLORD			PRINTED IN U.S.A.

EASTERN
EUROPE

Cultures and Costumes Series:

EASTERN EUROPE

CHRIS McNAB

MASON CREST PUBLISHERS

www.masoncrest.com

Mason Crest Publishers Inc.
370 Reed Road
Broomall, PA 19008
(866) MCP-BOOK (toll free)
www.masoncrest.com

First printing 2002

1 2 3 4 5 6 7 8 9 10

Library of Congress Cataloging-in-Publication Data available

ISBN 1-59084-441-6

Printed and bound in Malaysia

Editorial and design by
Amber Books Ltd.
Bradley's Close
74–77 White Lion Street
London N1 9PF

Project Editor: Marie-Claire Muir
Designer: Hawes Design
Picture Research: Lisa Wren

Picture Credits:
All pictures courtesy of Amber Books Ltd, except the following:
Mary Evans Picture Library: 18.

ACKNOWLEDGMENT
For authenticating this book, the Publishers would like to thank
Robert L. Humphrey, Jr., Professor Emeritus of Anthropology,
George Washington University, Washington, D.C.

Contents

Eastern Europe has undergone much change since 1989, including the breakup of the former Soviet Union and the birth of new independent states. The region's major cities, such as Prague, Vienna, and Budapest, have, at various times, been major centers of European culture.

Estonia

Latvia

Lithuania

Belarussia

Poland

Czech Republic

Slovakia

Ukraine

Austria

Moldova

Hungary

Slovenia

Romania

Croatia

Bosnia Herz.

Yugoslavia

Bulgaria

Albania

FYR Macedonia

Introduction

Nearly every species in the animal kingdom adapts to changes in the environment. To cope with cold weather, the cat adapts by growing a longer coat of fur, the bear hibernates, and birds migrate to a different climatic zone. Only humans use costume and culture—what they have learned through many generations—to adapt to the environment.

The first humans developed their culture by using spears to hunt the bear, knives and scrapers to skin it, and needles and sinew to turn the hide into a warm coat to insulate their hairless bodies. As time went on, the clothes humans wore became an indicator of cultural and individual differences. Some were clearly developed to be more comfortable in the environment, others were designed for decorative, economic, political, and religious reasons.

Ritual costumes can tell us about the deities, ancestors, and civil and military ranking in a society, while other clothing styles can identify local or national identity. Social class, gender, age, economic status, climate, profession, and political persuasion are also reflected in clothing. Anthropologists have even tied changes in the hemline length of women's dresses to periods of cultural stress or relative calm.

In 13 beautifully illustrated volumes, the *Cultures and Costumes: Symbols of their Period* series explores the remarkable variety of costumes found around the world and through different eras. Each book shows how different societies have clothed themselves, revealing a wealth of diverse and sometimes mystifying explanations. Costume can be used as a social indicator by scientists, artists, cinematographers, historians, and designers—and also provide students with a better understanding of their own and other cultures.

ROBERT L. HUMPHREY, JR., Professor Emeritus of Anthropology,
George Washington University, Washington, D.C.

Nobility and Aristocracy

During the first centuries of the Christian era, the nobility of Eastern Europe often dressed little better than its wealthier peasants. Soon, however, the region experienced a revolution in religion and culture that transformed the appearance of its elite.

Four forces in particular transformed the clothing of Eastern Europe's nobles and aristocrats: the decline of the Roman Empire in the third century; the birth of the Byzantine Empire in the fourth century; the invasion of tribes from Asia and northern Russia in the early medieval period; and the political alliances made between European countries from the 16th century onwards. With each of these events, the wealthy and powerful of the Eastern European countries altered their appearances to match their new social and cultural lives.

Costumes of the Nobles

During the first 400 years of the Roman Empire (c. 27 B.C.–A.D. 395), most of Europe was divided into local tribes and communities rather than the countries

These are typical costumes worn by Lithuanian and Polish nobles during the 16th century. The standard overgarment for men was the long coat, called a *joupane*, but a sleeveless type, called a *choupa*, was also worn.

that we know today. The largest ruling class was the **Slavs**. The Slavic people have their prehistoric origins in Asia, but during the second and third millennia B.C., they migrated into Eastern Europe. Once there, they divided into tribes, and each tribe had its own ruling class or group.

During this period, most nobles looked fairly similar to the local commoners. The tribal leaders of Hungary, Russia, and the Ukraine, for example, all wore costumes suited to their nomadic lifestyle on horseback. A shirt and wide pants were worn by both sexes, as was a long woolen tunic tied at the waist with a leather belt. Boots and caps made from felt gave warmth and protection to the feet and head, respectively.

What distinguished nobles from commoners was the quality of their clothing. In Russia, all people wore fur, but noble or wealthy individuals would be clad in the best ermine, sable, marten, beaver, otter, or lynx. By contrast, poorer people would wear the more common furs: wolf, bear, sheepskin, fox, or hare. The fine furs of the nobility sent a clear message of their high status, particularly as fur itself was often used as a form of currency in ancient Russia. Nobles also had clothing of brighter coloration. Women's costumes in particular featured striking shades of gold, yellow, green, and red. Jewelry would be made from finely worked bone, bronze, gold, or silver and was often inlaid with precious gems.

Male Tribal Leaders

Each tribe lived in constant danger from other tribes and, as the male tribal leaders provided practical military leadership to the tribe, they often had a military appearance. Swords in particular distinguished noblemen, as peasants were more commonly armed with daggers and basic agricultural tools or weapons. A metal brooch from fourth-century Hungary depicts a nobleman on horseback firing a bow and arrow. He is wearing a knee-length **doublet** pulled in at the waist with a leather belt, which holds a sword scabbard. He has high leather riding boots and his costume is decorated with small metal brooches.

The Rise of Byzantium

In the first centuries of the first millennium A.D., Rome controlled most of Europe, large sections of North Africa, and much of the Middle East, and its power seemed unassailable. However, by the fourth century A.D., its power was waning. Invading European and Asian tribes took back many of Rome's imperial conquests. Constantine, the Roman Emperor, realized that the Empire was under threat, and so he created a second capital in what is today Istanbul, Turkey. The new city was renamed **Constantinople** in A.D. 330, but had been previously known as Byzantium. This name is now used by historians to label the eastern section of the Roman Empire as the "Byzantine empire," which hinged around Constantinople and lasted for 11 centuries.

Between Worlds

Byzantium sat between the Oriental and Western worlds. Its citizens combined the simplistic long robes and togas seen around Rome with the vivid colors of garments worn in Egypt and Syria. Byzantium began trading with Eastern Europe just as the Roman Empire began to collapse, so Byzantine styles were adopted. Eastern European

This brooch was part of the riding outfit of a Polish noble. Precious stones inlaid in jewelry became particularly fashionable in the 17th century.

rulers imitated the clothes they saw at the Byzantine court. The kings and queens of Serbia, for example, began to wear a long, heavy gown called a *saccoz* that was purple or black in color and had sleeves that gathered at the wrists. Up until the 16th century, Byzantine emperors wore the same style of clothing.

Byzantine Style Influences

The Byzantine influence upon Eastern European dress was felt in other costumes as well. Silk became a more important cloth and was worn only by the rich, and royal costumes became heavier in decoration than those that had been worn by earlier nobles. Bulgarian aristocrats started wearing a special tunic usually worn by their equivalents in Byzantium. This long garment fell down to the knees or feet, was fastened at the right shoulder, and was highly decorated with braids and pearls. The Byzantine influence also changed the shape of pants: they became tighter, narrower, and reached down to the feet—the traditional Eastern European versions usually stopped at the calves.

In every Eastern European country, the influence of Byzantium transformed the dress of the nobility. The only exception to this was a brief period—around the 10th and 11th centuries—in which Christianity entered Eastern Europe. Christianity had traditionally distrusted highly ornamented clothing, and so, for a time, many nobles resorted to the plainer clothing of the past. However, the colorful traditions eventually made a comeback.

The Collapse of Byzantium

During the 10th and 11th centuries, the Byzantine empire started to fall into decline, and the various countries that made up the empire began to fight among themselves. The territories, including the Holy Land, were also under threat from powerful Muslim armies. As an act of rescue, European forces marched down into the Middle East to defend against the invaders, and entered into a series of wars that became known as the **Crusades**. The Christian Crusaders actually did more harm than good, pillaging many Byzantine lands and murdering many of the inhabitants they were supposed to be helping. In 1453, Byzantium fell to a massive Turkish army, and its influence in the world came to an end.

New Influences

The collapse of Byzantium meant that the way was open to new influences in Eastern European clothing. The Turks continued their expansion into Eastern Europe, with Muslim culture entering into countries such as Serbia and Bulgaria. Even countries that stayed Christian received some Islamic influences in many realms, including their dress. Polish nobles, for example, towards the end of the 15th century, began wearing a Persian garment called a **kontoush** together with a colored undergarment called a **joupane**. The *kontoush*'s neckline was cut low, to reveal the *joupane* underneath, and the sleeves were slashed for most of their length. The slashes also revealed the sleeves of the *joupane*. Polish nobility also wore cylindrical fur hats of the same style as those worn by Persian lords.

The Caftan

Persia and the Middle East were not the only influences on Eastern European costume after the fall of the Byzantine Empire. In the 13th century, the feared Mongol leader Genghis Khan swept across China and Russia and into Eastern Europe with an army of over

This outlandish figure of the Russian court wears a cloak and apron fringed with leather tassels.

150,000 warriors. Besides death and destruction, they brought with them the long, flowing robe known as the *caftan* (the Turkish invaders had also had a version of this item of dress). *Caftans* became popular among nobility in places such as Poland and Russia and remain so to this day in certain forms of traditional costume.

Eastern and Western Influences

The Turkish and Mongol invasions were undoubtedly cataclysmic events in Europe's history, but they also opened up international trade routes between the East and West. Silks from the Orient began to pour into Eastern and Western Europe and became more common materials for royal and noble clothing.

By the 15th and 16th centuries, the Turkish and Mongol empires had begun to collapse, and they steadily retreated to their homelands. They left behind them a Europe more integrated by trade, but also more geographically volatile. Russia went on to create its own empire. Between the 15th and 18th centuries, it acquired much Eastern European territory, including large portions of Poland, Estonia, Lithuania, Belorussia, the Ukraine, and the Crimea.

This volatile situation meant that Eastern European leaders and nobles came into contact with many styles of Eastern and Western European clothing. For example, 16th-century Slovakian nobles adopted the Hungarian *mente*—a long, decorated coat—as the national dress, and Lithuanians and Ukrainians donned Polish clothing in the 17th century.

Belarussia

In 16th-century Belarussia, the nobility borrowed items of clothing from the Poles, Lithuanians, Latvians, and Ukrainians, and also from Western nations such as Germany, France, and Austria. In the cities, landlords and aristocracy wore Western-style ropes made out of heavy, valuable cloths, and decorated with gold and silver **embroidery** and precious gems.

By the 17th century, the Belarussian aristocracy wore a vivid mix of local and international styles. In general, the silhouettes of the clothing lost the looseness of the native dress and became tighter fitting, matching the style of the Western Renaissance costume.

The long outer robes worn by Polish royalty of the 15th and 16th centuries were known as *zupan* or *kontuz* and were often lined with fur. The male figures carry an orb and scepter to signal authority.

Western Influences

Western influence permeated more countries than just Belarussia. In Croatia, aristocratic ladies wore long white satin ropes, aprons of exquisite lace, and sable-lined red velvet cloaks, imitating the style of the Empress of Austria.

In Poland, the court of the Vasa Kings (1521–1818) wore Spanish-style clothing. For men, this meant a short, close-fitting padded jacket known as a doublet and tight breeches; for women, dresses were worn over the farthingale, a hoop-shaped petticoat under the dress that made the skirt flare outward. Both sexes wore a ruff, a circle of frilled material around the neck. The court's imitation of Western clothing annoyed some Polish nobles, however, and in defiance they stuck strictly to Polish national dress, wearing the fur ***kolpak*** hat and the long *kontoush*.

Keeping Ethnic Styles Alive

Despite such acts of resistance, from the 17th century onward, the clothing of Eastern Europe became subject to the whims and fancies of fashion. While

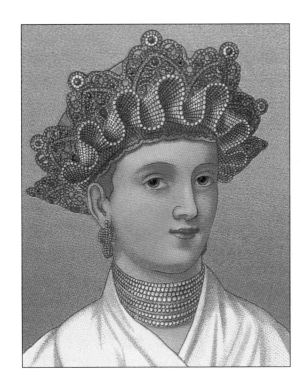

items of national dress made occasional appearances, in general, it was only the peasantry who kept ethnic styles alive. One Polish writer in the 17th century remarked, "How many continuously changing styles I remember in frocks, caps, boots,

Slaves in the Russian court would dress ornately to symbolize the status of their owners. This headdress has a fluted brim over the forehead and is decorated with rubies, sapphires, pearls, and topaz.

This slave headdress features a large crown heavily decorated with precious stones. All such headdresses were known as *tschepatz*, and their styles were derived from the clothing of European nobility.

swords, harnesses, and in every other kind of military garment and household utensils, as well as in house styles, gestures, walking and greeting habits! The outfits which I bought abroad would have lasted my whole lifetime—even my children would have profited by them—had they not gone out of fashion and become unstylish in a year or less."

Polish Crowns

Originally worn by chieftains of tribes, crowns were worn in Poland as symbols of aristocratic status from the early medieval period onwards. They soon became a mark of royalty, and from 1283 on, ordinary citizens were forbidden from wearing any crown of valuable or decorated metal. In 1792, an inspection of the Royal Treasury of Poland listed five royal crowns. These crowns, along with many other exquisite pieces of jewelry, were locked away in sealed chests in Wawel Castle in Krakow. In 1794, Prussian invaders occupied the city and discovered the valuable items. King Frederick William II of Prussia stole the crowns and other treasures and moved them to Germany; first to Berlin, then to Konigsburg. In Konigsburg in 1809, many of the jewels were destroyed, melted down for their gold after their precious stones had been removed. From then to the present day, Poland has been recovering any items not destroyed.

Ecclesiastical Dress

The religious costume of all of Europe is founded on its two major religions: Judaism and Christianity. However, Eastern Europe founded its own forms of ecclesiastical dress, distinct from those of Western Europe.

Judaism is possibly the world's oldest religion. Its theology is centered on the **Old Testament** of the Bible and a legal work known as the **Talmud**, a text that gives rules for everyday living. The Jewish people originated in the Middle East, in the territories of Israel. The **Diaspora**—the migration of Jewish peoples outside of Israel—began in the eigth century B.C. By the first century A.D., Judaism was heading northward into Europe and eventually spread to the **Balkans**, Russia, Poland, and Western Europe, where major communities of Jews were established.

Jewish Clerical Dress

The style of Jewish priestly vestments has remained remarkably constant since ancient times. In the **Middle Ages**, a rabbi in Poland would have been instantly

An Orthodox priest delivers a blessing. He wears the *kamelavkion*, a cylindrical black hat with a long black monastic veil. These hats were, and are, usually worn by monks, bishops, and church dignitaries.

recognizable to Jewish people anywhere in Europe. The situation changed only in the 19th century, when Jewish reformers allowed clerics to dress in a similar manner to Protestant religious figures. The reformers introduced a plain black gown and a round black hat as the standard dress of rabbis and cantors (the officials who lead the singing and prayers in the synagogue).

Dressing for Ceremonial Duties and Daily Prayer

Three items of costume in particular were (and still are) worn by Jewish Eastern European rabbis when performing ceremonial duties, and also by men dressing for daily prayer: the *tefillin*, the *tzitzit*, and the *tallit*. *Tefillin* are small black boxes made of hide that contain folded sections of Jewish scriptures. These boxes are worn in the center of the forehead and on the wrist and tied in place with leather thongs. *Tefillin* are meant to act as reminders about the appropriate ways of living a religious life. *Tzitzit* are fringes, or tassels, worn in obedience to a commandment in the Book of Numbers 15:39: "It shall be to you a tassel to look upon and remember all commandments of the Lord, and do them." On the rabbis' clothing, the tassels hung down from the hem of the outer robe. During times of persecution, however, rabbis hung the tassels from inner garments that were not exposed to public view. The *tallit* is a prayer shawl worn by the rabbi in the synagogue for morning and afternoon service and by all male worshippers for just the morning service. Made of either silk or wool, it is white with colorful decoration and fringes. Although

Polish Catholic monks of the 16th century wore voluminous habits. They tended to be in somber browns and blacks, but more colorful versions were prevalent in Eastern Europe, especially Russia.

today the *tallit* is usually worn like a scarf, prior to the 20th century, it was always wrapped closely around the head.

An ancient Jewish law stipulates that a Jewish male must not walk more than 6 feet (2 m) without a headcovering. To conform to this law, Jewish males have traditionally worn a skullcap (called a *kippah*), a small circular cap that is pinned into the hair and often worn all day long.

Christian Styles

Ancient Jewish traditions of ecclesiastical dress are still alive today, but Christianity has taken a more varied route in terms of clothing. Each individual Christian church, sect, and organization has developed its own styles since the birth of Christianity 2,000 years ago.

Between the 4th and 11th centuries A.D., there were two main religious powers in the Christian world. In Western Europe, there was the Holy Roman Empire. Its capital was Rome, and it practiced what we know today as the Roman Catholic faith. In Eastern Europe—particularly the Balkans and Russia—and the Middle East was the Eastern Roman Empire, more commonly known as the Byzantine empire, after its capital,

These Catholic monks are in typical liturgical dress. The circular haircut, known as the "tonsure," derives from the ancient Roman practice of shaving the heads of slaves—the priests are slaves to Christ.

Byzantium (later renamed Constantinople). This empire was dominated by the religion of Eastern Orthodoxy.

The Orthodox Churches

Originally, the two empires practiced the same brand of faith. The Byzantine empire, however, grew extremely powerful by A.D. 1000, whereas the Roman Empire had gone into significant decline. Byzantine religion looked more towards Greek and Oriental styles of worship and theology rather than the Western philosophies of Rome. Byzantium spread its own brand of Christianity throughout much of Eastern Europe, with Bulgaria, much of the Balkans, and Russia coming under Orthodox faith in the ninth century. Many countries formed their own brands of Orthodox religion, such as the Greek Orthodox, Russian Orthodox, and Ukrainian Orthodox churches.

When the Byzantine empire was founded in A.D. 330, church clothing was no longer influenced by contemporary styles and tended to be less fashion-conscious than the garments worn previously, which did not

A church elder in Russia would wear a hat of velvet or of fine fur, such as sable, mink, or arctic fox. This hat features a small brass bell tied over the forehead to mark its ceremonial function.

distinguish priests from the general public. Their costume consisted of a tunic, leggings, leather shoes, and a jacket. During the fourth and fifth centuries, however, Church authorities started to enforce a dedicated dress for priests and clerics. By the seventh century, church clothing was detached from fashion and tended to be less fashion-conscious than the early church garments had been.

A typical Byzantine Greek bishop of the 10th century wore an ankle-length *sticharion*, a simple tunic crossed over and tied at the waist. Over this he would wear a sleeveless outer garment known as a *chasuble* and a decorated scarf called a *pallium*. The *pallium* would often feature little pieces of lead attached to the ends, to make them hang down straight. More senior church figures of the same period had elaborately decorated outfits. A **Patriarch** would don the same clothing as the bishop, but might add the stunning *epitracheliom*; a **stole** made of a shimmering golden fabric and patterned with crosses and rectangles.

Clerical Costume in the Ukrainian Orthodox Church

Byzantine ecclesiastical clothing set the tone for Orthodox dress throughout Eastern Europe, from Greece to northern Russia. Typical items of clothing worn by **deacons**, priests, and bishops in the Ukrainian Orthodox Church, and which are still worn today, included the *sticharion*, a long tunic with loose sleeves that reached down to the ankles. The *sticharion* was tied together with a *zone*, a belt symbolizing strength. This simple garment represented a pure life dedicated simply to God. Worn over the *sticharion* by bishops was the *sakkos*, an outer garment that represented Christ's own coat, reputed to have healing properties. The *epimanika* was a set of additional cuffs worn around the wrists, to represent the binds tying the hands of Jesus Christ at his crucifixion.

A stole worn by deacons, the *orarion* was often embroidered with the Ukrainian words for "Holy, Holy, Holy." Unlike the straight-hanging Byzantine version, this Ukrainian scarf would be fashioned into a cross shape, passing from under the right arm to the top left-hand shoulder.

The *epitrachelion* was the priests' stole, worn as a symbol of church authority. It fitted around the neck like a scarf, was joined at the chest with hooks, and hung down to the knees. The *phelonion* was an outer cape worn by priests to symbolize good character and moral virtue. A diamond-shaped piece of strong material that was hung over the neck to sit over the right thigh, the *nabedrenyk* usually featured a cross as decoration and represented the protection provided by God's word.

The bishop's stole was called an *omophorion*. It was usually broader in width than that worn by lesser church officials. Most bishops would hang a cross over the stole in the center of the chest. Bishops would also wear a miter, a crown heavily decorated with embroidery, with a cross on the top, to demonstrate authority. During processions, bishops wore very long black capes called *mandyas* and a tall, cylindrical hat covered by a black veil called a *kamelavkion*. They would also carry a long staff to symbolize their authority. At the head of the staff would be two serpents looking at an orb and a cross. Finally, the *encolpia* were two medallions that were worn around the neck, one with an icon of Jesus Christ and the other depicting the Virgin Mary.

The *Dikerion* and the *Trikerion*

Since the earliest periods in Christian history, the *dikerion*, a double-branched candlestick, and the *trikerion*, a triple-branched candlestick, have been used by Orthodox priests during services. The *dikerion* represents the belief that there were two aspects of Jesus Christ's nature: human and divine. The three branches of the *trikerion* symbolize the three elements of God in Christianity: the father (God himself), the Son (Jesus Christ), and the Holy Spirit (the presence of God in the world). Both candlesticks are used to give blessings over individuals and congregations during services.

Modern Variations

Dress is not the only thing that has distinguished Orthodox priests in Eastern Europe throughout the ages. A member of the Orthodox clergy will also typically have long hair and a beard, both of which he is forbidden to cut. In the run-up to his ordination, a candidate for priesthood in the Orthodox Church will make the following promise: "I promise to wear the clothing appropriate to my priestly rank, not to cut my hair, nor my beard."

Holding on to Tradition

In recent years, there has been much controversy in the Orthodox Church as certain members of clergy have started to wear Western-style clerical dress, including a simple business suit. Most Orthodox officials are eager to stop this. In the Russian Orthodox Church, there is currently a rule stating: "None who is counted with the clergy should dress inappropriately, when in the city, nor when traveling. Each should use the attire that was appointed for clergy members. If someone breaks this rule, may he be deprived of serving for one week." This rule stems from the feeling that the traditional way of

The miter—the tall headdress worn by the bishop (right)—emerged from the 12th century. By the 15th century, miters were even studded with diamonds.

An Eastern Orthodox priest conducts a ceremony in a Russian peasant church. He wears a highly decorated *phelonion* (cape) over a plain white *sticharion* (tunic). The scarf-like item at the front is the *epitrachelion*.

dressing separates priests from the rest of humankind. Certainly, Orthodox ecclesiastical dress is one of the most recognizable religious uniforms in the world.

Roman Catholic Ecclesiastic Vestments

Like Orthodox priests, **Roman Catholic** priests initially wore the clothing of everyday fashions. In 572, however, at a meeting in Portugal called the Council of Braga, a law was passed requiring priests to wear an ankle-length tunic called a *vestis talaris*. This law affected priests in all corners of Europe, from Britain to Germany. However, it took longer to catch on in Eastern Europe, because

Christianity was slower to develop in these regions. Between the fourth and the ninth centuries, the Roman Catholic Church began laying down laws regarding **liturgical** dress that influenced the dress of Western clergy.

From the ninth century onwards, the dress of all Catholic clergy in Europe was effectively decided by the lawmakers in Rome. Nonetheless, the clothing of Eastern European Roman Catholics developed in a slightly different form than that of Western Europe. Eastern European vestments are fewer in number from their Western counterparts, but the two have several key items in common: an undertunic known as an *alb*, a *cincture* (belt), a sleeveless outer chasuble worn for **Mass**, a stole, and a **pallium**. More unusual Eastern European features included a veil that covered the face and a hat shaped like a tiara or turban. Other unusual Roman Catholic Eastern European dress items are derived from an Oriental Orthodox background. For example, Greek bishops, like Orthodox clergy, wear the *sakkos*.

Islamic Influences

Islam is very much a minority religion in Eastern Europe, but it has nonetheless had an impact on the dress of certain nationalities. Perhaps most influenced by Islam are the former territories of Yugoslavia, which are 20 percent Muslim, and Albania, which is 90 percent Muslim. Both countries fell under Turkish rule in the Middle Ages, and so began a connection with Islam. Today, several items of Islamic influence can be seen in some Eastern European clothing. In Croatia, one can see **bolero jacket**s with gold braids, circular hats that resemble the Turkish *fez*, and Middle Eastern-style leather slippers. In Bosnia-Herzegovina, men can be seen wearing turbans and gold waistcoats with ceremonial Islamic daggers. Albanian men wear white felt *fezzes*, and Albanian children often wear Oriental-style leather shoes.

Military Uniforms

In most Eastern European countries, proper military uniforms did not develop until the 17th and 18th centuries. When they did finally emerge, they were among the most elaborate and stylish uniforms in the world.

In medieval Europe, most countries did not have formal, professional armies. Rather, kings and lords would often recruit their armies as and when they were needed, from either the local population or by employing foreign mercenaries.

Knights and Heavy Cavalry

The only true military professionals were the warrior horsemen: the knights and heavy cavalry. Shining suits of armor instantly distinguished these ranks. Full armor consisted of a metal bodysuit that was hinged at the body's natural joints and topped with a helmet that covered the face, skull, and neck entirely. The role of the knight and heavy cavalry was to charge into the midst of the enemy, destroying its ranks and organization and throwing it into confusion.

Eastern European soldiers of the 16th century: the Hussar on the left wears metal armor and helmet, while the Russian cavalryman on the right has a chain-mail vest over a long cloth jacket.

Polish Military Dress

In the 15th century, Poland reformed its military force, leading to the development of four separate degrees of armor protection, designated according to rank. At the top of the ladder was the knight, who would receive full armor. Beneath the knight was the lancer, who would be mounted on horseback and armed with a long spear. The lancer was dressed in "half-armor," usually a helmet and pieces of armor for his arms and legs. Of a much lower rank was the crossbowman. He would fight using the **crossbow** as his weapon and would wear only a *cuirass*: a breastplate and back protector tied together around his torso. Finally, there was the swordsman, a soldier armed only with his sword and protected by nothing more than a shield.

Eastern European Infantry

In all Eastern European armies, from the start of the Middle Ages to the late 16th century, beneath the ranks of the mounted soldiers would be little more than a rabble of infantry. Infantry were usually peasants, and could not afford sophisticated uniforms. They dressed as they would in the fields: in leather or felt boots, brown or black pants, a tunic made from rough material, and a simple cloth cap.

The Crusaders

The Crusades were a series of medieval military expeditions made primarily by Western European armies in an attempt to drive the Muslims out of the Holy Land. These expeditions took place over the 11th, 12th, and 13th centuries. Crusading armies would march thousands of miles down from Britain, France, Germany, Belgium, and various other countries to fight the Muslim invaders.

A common uniform was needed to differentiate the Crusaders from their Muslim opponents. The solution was a long white garment that was worn over armor, known as a *surcoat*. The *surcoat* not only defined the Crusaders as such; it could also be decorated in the national and regional symbols of its wearer.

Three Polish soldiers of the 1880s dressed in the uniforms of the royal guard. The first two soldiers (from left to right) wear tall felt bonnets called *kulah*, which featured a long plume of feathers.

Standing Army Uniforms

Towards the end of the 17th century, military service had begun to change. More and more countries realized that they needed regular armies to protect their nations, as opposed to recruiting soldiers only when they were needed. The creation of "standing armies"—permanent armies made up of full-time soldiers—had a huge effect on the appearance of military uniforms.

Between the end of the 17th century and the beginning of the 20th century, Eastern European countries established national uniforms for their new standing armies. These uniforms served several purposes. First, they defined which regiment or division a soldier belonged to and so helped commanders on the battlefield organize their troops. They were also a statement of national pride. Finally, they were designed to help the soldier fight more efficiently and effectively, as their systems of belts, straps, and pouches, worn over the uniform, held weaponry and ammunition. These systems became still more important when firearms became the standard infantry weapon during the 17th and 18th centuries and soldiers needed to carry cartridges and musket balls.

Hungarian Infantry and Cavalry

Today's armies wear camouflaged uniforms, designed to make soldiers as inconspicuous as possible. By contrast, in the 17th and 18th centuries, military

Three medieval Polish soldiers: most soldiers wore the long *joupane* (tunic). Originally, these were gray, but throughout the medieval period, they changed to reddish and green colors.

uniforms were bright and ostentatious. Hungary formed a national army in 1848–1849 and used its national dress as the basis of the military uniform. Infantry and artillery officers initially wore long, dark-brown jackets called *atilla* jackets. These jackets featured red braided fittings for the regular soldiers and gold ones for the officers. Officers also wore a red, white, and green sash tied around their waists and light blue pants with red stripes running down their legs. Regular soldiers had pants that matched their *atilla* jackets. The standard form of headgear was a *shako*, a peaked cap featuring a **cockade** with the Hungarian national colors.

Although infantry uniforms could be highly decorated, they were usually nothing compared to the uniforms worn by cavalry. A Hungarian hussar would wear a short, dark-blue jacket covered in white metal buttons and featuring a bright-red collar. Over this he would wear a fur-lined **pelisse**, also dark blue in color. His pants would be gray breeches with red stripes running down the sides, which would fit into his calf-length riding boots. His *shako* would be similar to that worn by an army soldier, but his would be wrapped in cords in the regimental colors and would sometimes feature a red feather standing high in the air.

Polish Infantry and Cavalry

The differences in uniforms between those on horseback and those on foot were just as marked in other Eastern European armies. In Poland, the regular infantry soldiers wore basic tunics, pants, and caps in the colors of the region from which their unit originated.

This Polish swordsman wears a crimson hooded cloak and felt boots. Red uniforms were only worn by the nobility, and the Polish word for crimson became an alternative term for "gentleman."

They were armed with a rifle and a combat ax called a *berdysz*. When not in use, the *berdysz* was strapped across the back using a belt. The hussars and dragoons that formed the cavalry could not have looked more different. Their costume consisted of a leather jacket covered with armor and a helmet with long eagle feathers stuck into it. Over his left shoulder, the cavalryman wore a tiger, leopard, or wolf skin tied into place by a metal buckle, and on the breastplate of his armor was an image of the Virgin Mary. The cavalry horses would be just as highly decorated: their saddles and bridles featured heraldic crests, and precious jewels were inlaid in the leather. A highly embroidered horse cloth would almost entirely obscure the animal beneath.

Russian Infantry

Russian infantry wore a peculiar form of clothing that first emerged in the middle of the 17th century. Between about 1650 and 1700, most infantry wore a long *caftan* that reached down to the ankles. The front of the *caftan* was

Uniforms and Civilian Dress

Military style had a big impact on civilian costume. Being a soldier became a mark of distinction among the nobility during the 17th century, and their clothing reflected military trends. The military *caftan*, for example, spread throughout most of Europe in the late 17th century and became a fashionable item of gentlemanly dress. At social events, a gentleman—particularly one who belonged to the cavalry tradition— would often wear a full-dress military uniform. Conversely, civilian fashions also influenced military uniforms. For example, powdered faces, artificial hair curls, and frilly lace cuffs and gaiters became part of the Russian officer's uniform in the mid-1700s as these items became fashionable in Russian society.

Four Polish knights of the 13th century. Metal body armor and helmets were worn in Poland between the 12th and the 18th centuries. The pointed helmet of the soldier on the left was a Slavic design.

heavily decorated with ornamental lace and colored braid, and the waist was tied with a braided and tasseled belt that was wrapped several times around the torso. Headgear was either a high helmet or a rather shapeless felt cap edged in fur. By the early 1700s, however, this uniform looked out-of-date when compared with other Eastern European armies. In 1720, a short green coat replaced the *caftan*, with breeches and stockings worn on the legs. The fur cap went out, and in came a variety of peaked, conical, and pointed caps adorned with braids, embroidery, and feathers.

World War I: A Turning Point

The flamboyant uniforms of the 17th, 18th, and 19th centuries began a fundamental change with the approach and arrival of World War I. By this time, military weaponry had reached lethal levels of efficiency. Machine guns, long-range artillery, and accurate rifles meant that anyone who could be seen easily on the battlefield would not survive for long. Furthermore, the days of

A cavalry officer of the Serbian Hussars in WWI, wearing a bright blue attila jacket with officer's gold braid, breeches, and riding boots. His cap has a gray cover to make him less conspicuous to snipers.

the horse-mounted cavalry were drawing to a close. In the first year of the war, Serbian and Austrian cavalry died by the thousands, their powerful horses a futile weapon against the hail of bullets and shells. The old days of the warrior were ending, and the years of industrial warfare had begun.

At the start of World War I, many European armies had already begun to put their soldiers in plain khaki or field-gray uniforms, because simple uniforms served better in the harsh climates of overseas colonies. Moreover, armies were growing massive in size, and it was too expensive to equip all soldiers with elaborate uniforms.

In Eastern Europe, some traditions died hard, particularly among cavalry and some of the older infantry regiments. The Hungarian hussars were one such unit. These soldiers wore bright blue tunics and pelisses, made even more visible by their red lacing and white fur edging. The peaked *shako* was even fitted with a large comb of fur at the front, making the soldier stand out even more. Although an impressive sight, a hussar dressed in such a way presented an easy target to soldiers armed with rifles. Gradually, these traditional uniforms were replaced on the battlefield by plain infantry uniforms, the full dress uniform only being worn on ceremonial occasions.

A Single Style

By the end of World War I, the traditions of elaborate uniforms in Eastern Europe had all but died out. Soldiers around the world became increasingly similar in appearance, the only thing distinguishing armies usually being the basic color of the uniform and the shape of the helmet. After World War II, camouflage was increasingly introduced, and today, this pattern adorns the standard uniforms of most of the world's armies, including those of Eastern Europe. Traditional uniforms are still worn by soldiers belonging to elite or venerable regiments on ceremonial occasions, and wearing such uniforms is a matter of great pride.

Yugoslavian Officers in World War II

The uniforms of the Eastern European armies in World War II were usually plain and almost completely devoid of ornamentation. There were some exceptions, however. The uniforms of officers in the Royal Yugoslav Army, for example, still retained some of the decorative features of their 19th-century precursors. The basic uniform consisted of a field-gray tunic belted at the waist with a leather belt and matching riding breeches with a scarlet stripe down the side of each leg. The breeches were tucked into a high pair of pull-on riding boots. Accompanying the tunic was an *aiguillette*, a thick gold braid that looped under the right armpit and crossed the chest. This braid hung down over the center buttons and terminated in two arrowlike metal fittings. The large shoulder boards displaying the wearer's rank were stitched in gold, with a red border, and the headdress was a field cap featuring the Yugoslavian cockade.

Peasant Life

Traditional forms of everyday peasant dress in Eastern Europe tended to peter out in the first decades of the 20th century. These styles of dress had reflected an older way of looking at the world and had considerable spiritual significance.

Eastern Europe is a place of dramatic physical contrasts: the southern region tends to be extremely mountainous—particularly the Balkans, Bulgaria, and Western Romania, through which the Carpathian Mountains run. Above the Carpathian Mountains, however, is a vast flatland of marshes, plains, and hilly forests known as the North European Plain. This flatland covers much of Eastern Europe, including Poland, the Ukraine, Belarussia, Lithuania, Latvia, Estonia, and Western Russia. Climates also vary tremendously in Eastern Europe. Greece, for example, enjoys tropical temperatures in the summer and mild winters. Northern Russia, by contrast, has mild summers but arctic-temperature winters.

Peasant clothing in Eastern Europe was much more than just protection against the weather. As peoples acquainted with the realities of agricultural existence, peasants dressed in ways that reflected their desires for health, fertile land, and spiritual safety.

A Russian family says a blessing before a meal. The women wear dresses with red decoration around the waistline and buttonholes, and red headresses. Red was thought to provide protection against evil spirits.

Colder Climates

Because of the vast differences in Eastern Europe's physical features, the costumes of its peasants, which were originally meant for daily life and work, varies according to region. Up in the Russian arctic, for example, live about 300,000 ethnic peoples of various tribes, including the Yakut, Chukchi, Nenet, and Yukaghir. For centuries, the frozen, flat, watery climate of this region has meant that fishing and reindeer herding were the primary occupations, and thus the traditional clothing was designed around these roles. Men wore close-fitting, knee-length boots made out of walrus or reindeer fur and featuring front panels decorated with embroidery and **appliqué**. The soles of these boots were constructed in strips of fur, the fur of each strip running in alternate directions to provide an ingenious non-slip sole. The same types of fur were used to make long robes, hooded to protect the face and braided to provide some decoration. Women's clothing was similar to men's, but more decorative. The coloration of all of the clothing involved a lot of red, as typically used in hunting societies.

Dinaric and *Pannonian* Styles

Although Eastern European peasant clothing differed from region to region, there were two basic styles of blouses and shirts: *dinaric* and *pannonian*. Blouses and shirts in the *dinaric* style, the more common of the two, were cut very straight and square, with wide, rectangular sleeves. The front **placket** was cut very deep, with embroidered motifs at its edges. A **gusset** was placed under each armpit, and the ends of the sleeves were usually decorated with embroidery or frills. *Pannonian* clothing is made up of panels of material gathered up toward a narrow neckline. The lines of the sleeves are curved and close on a narrow cuff. *Pannonian* dress tended to be more common in the southern regions of Eastern Europe and Poland, whereas the *dinaric* style featured heavily in Russian costume.

Two styles of hat were worn by Russian peasants in the 1800s: either thick fur caps made of animal skin or fur-lined felt hats, as seen here. Felt has the advantage of staying soft even in intense cold.

Bulgarian Peasant Costume

Now we jump to the opposite end of Eastern Europe: Bulgaria. This country is principally an agricultural society, and its climate is temperate, with cold, wet winters and hot summers. Bulgarian peasant costume contrasted greatly with that of the arctic Russians. Both men and women wore loose tunics or blouses made of white linen, both of which were ideal for keeping cool in the hot summers, and also for displaying fine needlework decoration. Over this, the women might wear a black cloth overdress with a white embroidered **chemise** underneath. The men usually wore white serge breeches with black embroidery, and over their tunics, a short-sleeved jacket with a cummerbund. Unlike the northern peoples' thick fur boots, footwear for Bulgarian peasants consisted of light, leather shoes or slip-on sandals that were laced up to the ankles. Headgear for men consisted of a cylindrical sheepskin hat known as a *tarboosh*; women wore a white head cloth called a *shamiya*.

Historical Influences and Religious Patterns

The contrast between Bulgarian and arctic Russian peasant dress was only one of the many contrasts in Eastern European clothing. Peasant dress varied from region to region—even from village to village. There have also been some major historical forces at work that have shaped Eastern European folk dress, the most significant of which is religion.

Particularly in terms of decoration, the greatest influence on the development of Eastern European peasant dress was the rise of the Orthodox Church. From about A.D. 800 onwards, as the faith of Byzantium began to spread among the Slavic peoples of Eastern Europe, the imagery of Eastern Christianity started to show up on peasant clothing.

Previously, the symbols, markings, and icons that were sewn, appliquéd, or embroidered onto peasant dress had more to do with superstition and magic than with organized religion. Typical decorative images included goddess symbols, the Tree of Life, figures of animals, and depictions of the sun.

Goddess Symbols

Goddess figures featured heavily in Eastern European dress. Usually, the goddesses were depicted in human form with their arms raised in worship or seated in a birthing position. In Russia, as well as in some parts of the Balkans, the goddess

The two Polish gentlemen in the center wear fine leather boots, signifying wealth, whereas the other figures, peasants, go either shoeless or wear simple rawhide moccasins bound with thongs.

was often depicted as a bird with a human face. Russian clothing in particular portrayed the bird-goddesses known as Sirine and Alconoste, mythological creatures that were believed to sing to those who had gone to paradise.

The Tree of Life

Trees were used to symbolize life, growth, health, fertility, and various other attributes essential to the survival of a tribe. A typical Tree of Life design on Eastern European dress showed a trunk branching out into many delicate branches, each containing vibrant, colored leaves, flowers, and buds. In places like Hungary, the tree was represented in the shape of a cross, as crossroads were

believed to possess a magical force. In the Ukraine and Bulgaria, tree images were combined with the shape of the goddess with upraised arms; these images were stitched onto the hems of skirts.

Hunting and Animal Images

For the peasants of many Eastern European countries, hunting was more than mere survival; it also signified the balance of life and death in nature. Accordingly, various hunting scenes were commonly seen in peasant dress. In Greece, domestic animals were depicted being attacked by lions or eagles in colorful appliqué and embroidery scenes. Isolated antlers and horns were depicted on tunics, dresses, and cloaks in most Eastern European countries, particularly those on the northern European plain, which relied on deer, caribou, and cattle for their existence. In Russia, Bulgaria, Romania, and Transylvania, women of the lowest peasant class wore horned headdresses; the horns were thought to connect them with the world of spirits.

Birds

Birds have powerful spiritual connotations in many religions. For example, the Book of Genesis tells us that it was a dove that brought the olive branch back to Noah to signify that the great flood had subsided. In Eastern Europe, bird images as clothing decoration tended to represent the spirit world or the idea of fertility.

The Sun

The sun was a natural image for clothing in Eastern Europe, where it had a particularly vital role in making crops grow. Images of the sun were often combined with images of animals. In Russia, for instance, woolen coats featured images of the sun as a galloping horse. In Slovakia, the sun was often depicted surrounded by birds and flowers; this pattern was typically sewn onto the sleeves of shifts or onto caps or headscarves. In the Balkans—especially

A variety of peasant costumes likely to be seen on the streets of a Polish town in medieval times. The woman on the left is wearing a headdress based on Western European styles of court costume.

Serbia and Croatia—the sun was stitched in dramatic red, blue, and green wool, and covered in images of horns and stars. In all cases, the sun was worn as a superstitious prayer to fertility and the divine.

Christian Motifs

From about A.D. 800, these pagan patterns were expanded upon with a new range of Christian motifs imported with the Eastern Orthodox Church. There are two different types of Christian art: narrative and iconic. Narrative art tells a story, while iconic art shows images that are important to a particular faith or belief. In Eastern Europe, stories from both the Old and **New Testament** theologies were often found embroidered in panels across shawls and headcoverings. Some of the most typical scenes show

Adam and Eve in the Garden of Eden, Jacob wrestling with the angel, and the Crucifixion.

The most important iconic decoration on Eastern European clothing was the cross. As soon as Christianity became widespread, the cross was used to embellish clothing. In Romania, a peculiar staggered-cross design was embroidered onto shirt and blouse sleeves, while in Bosnia, Yugoslavia, the shawls of village women featured a large, bright cross.

Pagan Remnants

The rural world from ancient times until the 20th century was one of spirits, curses, and the worship of long-dead ancestors. While the spread of the Orthodox faith brought new religious life to Eastern Europe, many of these old superstitions persisted. Celtic and Slavic peoples continued to perform rites of sacrifice to ancient ancestors, asking them to bless crops, families, and animals with health and fertility. Many Eastern European peoples also had legends of ghosts, demons, and evil spirits, against which they needed protection. Slavic

These Russian peasant ladies are wearing dresses of gold brocade with tasseled hems. The matching brocade headdresses indicate they are married.

and Hungarian communities, for instance, feared blood-sucking vampires (from which the legends of Count Dracula emerged).

Magical Properties

Clothes had an important role in the superstitions of Eastern European peasantry. Certain symbols and patterns were considered to have magical properties and thus were featured heavily on coats, blouses, dresses, and shawls, as well as jewelry. Generally, any decorative features on clothing were gathered around openings in the clothing or near exposed parts of the body. Cuffs, collars, buttonholes, hems, and seams were thought to be vulnerable to invasion by spirits, and so these points were heavily embroidered with "protective" patterns.

Seams were spiritually "held together" by bright stitching (usually red, white, and green) that zigzagged across the two pieces of material. In parts of Russia, for example, the necklines of women's blouses were decorated with a bright "V" pattern of embroidery known as the "guardian of the breasts" (breasts were considered sacred and in need of protection because of their role in feeding newborn infants). Eastern European peasant women would also wear headscarves and heavy aprons to protect their bodies from spirits, even if they were not actually involved in manual work. In Greece, a decorated apron was believed to have the power to induce a woman to give birth if it was thrown over her stomach. Women's hair was usually covered by a headscarf, because it was believed to have the magical power to seduce men and cause them to behave like lunatics.

Patterns and Motifs

Decorative patterns and motifs on clothing made their wearers feel more secure in a world of constant spiritual danger. Certain patterns and symbols recur across the Eastern European region. One such symbol was the triangle. Triangles promoted female fertility, while their sharp angles were supposed to blind the eyes of evil spirits. These shapes also represented the mystical **Trinity** of the Father, Son, and Holy Spirit, and so were worn by Christians as well.

Other common decorative symbols included circles and celestial images. Circles tended to represent the sun and moon—the forces signifying light and dark and life and death to Eastern European peasantry. Celestial images, such as stars and crescents, also evoked these elemental forces and gave protection from spirit forces.

Spiral patterns were originally marked in the earth in the Middle East to purify it before a building was erected. This use of spiral patterns migrated to Eastern Europe, where their appearance on clothing was thought to sanctify its wearer. Spiral patterns on door thresholds are still common today in Hungary and Czechoslovakia.

Peasant dress from the agricultural region of Torjok, central Russia. The man is dressed simply, whereas the woman has an outfit made entirely of striped silk with a slashed-sleeve outer garment.

Polish Peasant Costume

The Polish climate can be extremely cold in the autumn and winter months. Polish peasant clothing reflected this reality, being both durable and warm. A typical item of clothing for both men and women was a short, sleeveless sheepskin jacket that was worn over a white linen shirt or blouse. The fur was worn on the inside, but was also on display around the jacket's edges, collar, sleeves, and pockets. Embroidery ran up the front panels of the jacket, depicting spirals, triangles, and zigzag patterns. For the winter, Polish peasants usually wore a similar jacket that was thigh-length, bulkier, and had long, padded sleeves. Footwear consisted of felt boots that were laced high up the ankle.

In pagan and Christian traditions, the numbers 3, 7, and 12 have sacred significance. Consequently, all of the patterns described were often repeated in multiples of these numbers.

Bright Colors

The wearing of bright colors was thought to be another means by which to ward off evil spirits and provide spiritual protection in Eastern Europe. Red, in particular, featured prominently in peasant clothing, from the Balkans to northern Europe, with its connotations of blood, vitality, and strength. Siberian costume was almost entirely decorated in red, and tribes such as the Tcheremiss and Mordu would sew large red eyes on their blouses and jackets to combat evil influences. In Romania, married women would use red ribbons to tie their aprons to their waists on Sundays—the same ribbon that had been used to tie themselves and their husbands together during their marriage ceremonies. In the mountains of Yugoslavia, herdsmen's jackets featured red seams and tassels for protection.

Clothing for Occasions

Every year, Eastern Europe is host to a rich pageant of festivals, holidays, and celebrations. Many of these occasions display the best examples of each region's clothing and show the full beauty of each national heritage. Festivals, holidays, pageants, and celebrations in Eastern Europe are the ideal occasions—sometimes the only occasions—for seeing the full splendor of national dress today.

Because Eastern Europe is so rich in history and culture, every country, region, town—even every village—seems to have its own festivals. All these events bring out the best in ethnic and national clothing. In Bulgaria, the International Folk Festival is held in Burgas every August and the Varna Summer International Festival is held in July. Lithuania has at least 13 major national festivals, including the Day of the Lithuanian Flag (January 1), Independence Day (February 16), Stork Day (March 25), and the Day of

Southern Eastern European peasant dress often had Oriental styles. The boy is wearing a Turkish-style *fez*, the man on the right has a Muslim turban and pointed Oriental shoes, and the woman's clothes reflect Turkish and Gypsy origins.

Lithuanian Warriors (November 23). All Eastern European countries celebrate Easter, though in very different ways. In the Ukraine, for example, on the last Sunday before Easter, pussy-willow branches are blessed in church on "Willow Sunday."

Lithuanian Festival Costume

Eastern European festival clothing has its roots in the costumes worn by peasants during the few holiday periods that occurred in their working year. In Lithuania, for example, prior to the 20th century, peasants would wear elaborate and highly decorated costumes for celebratory and religious events, such as Easter or the summer solstice. On these occasions, women would wear long, handwoven skirts with bright blue stripes; white blouses with blue-embroidered cuffs and collars; short, sleeveless jackets; brightly colored, tasseled aprons; and small, cloth crowns decorated in blues and reds. Men would wear outfits to match those of the women. These outfits consisted of blue and white striped pants with decorated ankles, colorful braided belts, white shirts, blue and red sleeveless jackets, and bright-red braided neckties.

At the end of the 19th century and the beginning of the 20th, Lithuania went through a political period in which it tried to create a national identity separate from its past as a country often invaded and occupied by others. The type of clothing described became established as official national costume rather than just local festival dress.

National Identities

During the 20th century, Western European and U.S. culture has steadily become dominant around the world, and national identities in clothing are constantly being eroded by popular Western fashions. To defend themselves against this trend, many Eastern European countries have made a determined effort to keep their traditional national costumes alive. This effort typically involves promoting the wearing of regional ethnic clothing, or even combining

A 19th-century Slavic Russian is dressed in the fine clothing of a married woman. Married women gathered their hair on top of their heads. The pointed headdress is called a *kokoschnik* meaning "cock's comb."

different regional elements into a single unified national outfit. The proliferation of ethnic dance groups around Europe in recent years has also helped to keep many traditional costumes alive.

Hungarian Festival Costume

The original inhabitants of Hungary were Slavic and Germanic, but in the ninth century, invaders from the east known as Huns and Magyars took over the country, establishing a kingdom in 1001. In the 16th century, Turkey took over. The Turks were eventually expelled, with the assistance of Austria, and Hungary became part of the Austro-Hungarian Empire. In the 20th century, Hungary spent over 40 years under Moscow-centered Communist control. Today, while Hungary is an independent nation, its festival dress—a striking mix of Eastern and Western styles—reflects the many different influences on its history.

Hungarian festival costume varies depending on the region. Generally, women wear highly decorated, wide skirts, layers of petticoats, and white blouses, all edged with fine lace. In the north, eight or nine starched petticoats might be worn under the skirt to make it flare out. In the west and the south, the basic festival dress for women consists of a cotton skirt covered with green, blue, and red floral patterns. Most regions feature a colorful fringed shawl, but in the southeast, this is omitted in favor of a high-necked blouse with elaborate lace panels down the front and around the collar.

Silver jewelry became particularly popular in Europe during the Middle Ages. This set of Hungarian equine jewelry uses flower, rosette, and foliage motifs made popular by the silver makers of Spain.

Male Hungarian national costume comes in two forms. For most festival occasions, men will wear *gatya*, a white calf-length pair of pants that are so broad they appear to be a skirt. These pants are paired with white shirts, black waistcoats, black aprons decorated with colored braids, and occasionally, a black hat featuring a high dome and a black ribbon edged with yellow. A plainer style of festival dress consists simply of black pants tucked into calf-length boots, worn with a white wide-sleeved shirt, a black waistcoat, and a black hat.

Ukrainian Festival Costume

Ukrainian national dress can be seen in festivals all over the world. Huge numbers of Ukrainian people have emigrated from their homeland—over 1.5 million

A Croatian male in ceremonial clothes wears a black felt hat with a yellow crown, a blue waistcoat common in the Balkans, and a white tunic. His bag features red tassels often applied to hunting clothing.

live in North America alone—but they have taken with them rich traditions in clothing. In both male and female dress, ornate embroidery is standard. The male costume is a white linen smock featuring green and yellow embroidery; scarlet, blue, or white pantaloons tucked into calf-length black or red boots; and a green sash tied around the middle of the waist. In winter months, an additional item is added to the festival costume: a sleeveless white linen jacket edged in black lamb's wool, and featuring black embroidery on the cuffs, pockets, and down the front.

Unlike the bulky Hungarian women's dress, the festival costume of Ukrainian women is much slimmer fitting. It usually consists of a short, narrow-woven wool skirt worn over a white petticoat that protrudes from the skirt's bottom. A white linen apron is often worn over the skirt to conceal an open-front seam. Worn on the upper body is a white linen blouse embroidered with floral motifs. This blouse will either have three-quarter length sleeves or fallen sleeves that flare at the wrists. A velvet or woolen sleeveless jacket in green, red, or blue is usually worn over the blouse. Finishing the outfit is a floral headdress adorned with several brightly colored ribbons that trail down the wearer's back.

Polish Festival Costume

Like the Ukraine, Poland has a history of many influences within its borders. Between 1772 and 1795, Poland was partitioned between Russia, Prussia, and Austria; it wasn't until 1918 that Poland finally declared its independence. This was brought about during World War I, which saw the Russians driven out of Poland by the Germans and Austrians in 1915, who in turn were defeated with the support of the U.S. and the Allies in 1918. In 1939, World War II broke out, and Poland was invaded by the Soviet Union and Nazi Germany. During the German occupation, almost all of Poland's three million Jews were slaughtered. After the war ended, Poland was put under Communist control, which lasted until 1990. Much of Poland's ethnic culture was destroyed under

Nineteenth-century Hungarians wearing full ceremonial dress. The man's hat features ribbons and fresh flowers, a common festival style. The woman has an ornate sleeveless overvest displaying traditional ethnic patterns.

these cruel regimes, but today the national dress nevertheless appears during festivals and ceremonial occasions. (The only place where ethnic dress is still worn daily is in a remote area of the Tatra Mountains).

Having existed under so many different regimes, Poland has varied traditions of festival and ethnic dress across its regions. Generally speaking, however, men's costumes tend to have a slightly military appearance. In the city of Krakow, men wear a long blue and red coat with tassels on the chest that is reminiscent of a hussar uniform. Along with this coat, long, baggy pantaloons are worn, tucked into calf-length riding boots. In some regions, rather than long coats, men wear short, sleeveless jackets edged in bright colors. This jacket is worn over a white linen shirt and tied with a multicolored sash around the waist. Headgear consists of a black felt hat with a narrow brim decorated with colored braid.

Polish women boast some of the most colorful ethnic costumes in all of Eastern Europe. In Lodicz, the women wear startlingly bright, striped skirts made from strips of brightly colored material and hemmed with floral designs.

The Polonaise

Among the Eastern European aristocracy and nobility, many costumes were developed in response to fashionable new dances. In Poland, one such dance was the Polonaise. The Polonaise developed in the 18th century from a walking dance known as the Chodnozy, which had been popular in the 17th century. The Polonaise has a similar rhythm to a waltz, and the dancers move slowly and elegantly around the floor while holding hands—but they never face each other.

Although the nobility of 18th-century Poland was starting to wear international fashions, it was felt that 17th-century Polish dress was more appropriate for the Polonaise. For men, this meant long, fur-lined overcoats (called *kontusz*) in bright colors with slit sleeves, fur hats decorated with feathers and jewels, high riding boots, and colorful silk belts. Later, during the 19th century, men would actually wear Polish military uniforms while performing the dance. Women performing the Polonaise wore either a feminine version of the male costume or a white skirt and low-cut blouse—an outfit with a distinctly French style. Evidence seems to suggest that men wore more traditional Polish clothing, while women opted for international fashions.

These floral designs are also present on the white blouse and sleeveless black waistcoat that completes this costume. In Krakow, the skirts are more reserved, but the waistcoats have large panels of beadwork and tassels to match the male costume. Depending on the region, women cover their heads with either a brightly colored headscarf or a floral headdress with ribbons.

Wedding Costumes

Before many traditional ceremonies declined in the late 20th century, festivals

These late 19th-century Russian children wear decorated aprons over their dresses. The traditional headscarf is wrapped around the entire neck to protect the wearer from dust.

were not the only events for which special clothing was worn in Eastern Europe. Weddings, engagements, funerals, births, and dances were just some of the other occasions requiring decorative or symbolic costume.

Weddings were possibly the most highly celebrated occasions in Eastern European towns and villages. Generally speaking, traditional ethnic festival dress was worn by the bride, groom, and congregation, but with some special additions and embellishments. In the Lowicz region of Poland, for example, brides would wear a large headdress made of freshly cut flowers. In this region—and in many others throughout Eastern Europe—a woman's power of attraction was believed to reside in her hair. Decorating a woman's hair heavily with flowers made it look beautiful, while also covered it up to protect her modesty and shield her from attracting other men. Once married, most women in traditional communities wore headscarves to symbolize their marital status.

Embroidery

Embroidery had a particular significance on Polish wedding outfits. Triangles—traditional symbols of fertility—were sewn onto wedding dresses to encourage the couple to produce many healthy children. The groom-to-be would often receive an embroidered waistcoat from his fiancée to wear on the day of the wedding. In Hungary, once a man reached marriageable age, he received a special woolen coat embroidered with flowers known as a *szür*. He would wear this coat throughout a courtship, and then at his wedding. It would also make an appearance at future festivals. In other places, such as in Montenegro, men were only allowed to wear embroidered clothes after they were married, and hence, considered full men.

Costumes for Birth

Births were another main event in Eastern European culture that required special clothing. In Bulgaria, the gown worn by a baby when it was born would receive a series of red stitches around the neck to symbolize that its wearer was now a member of humanity. Other communities would embroider protective coats to shield the mother and newborn baby from harm. In crowded peasant houses in Czechoslovakia, the mother would be separated by an embroidered bed curtain called a *kutnice*—in some cases, knives or garlic were hung from this curtain to keep away evil spirits. In Hungary, as soon as a child was born, its grandmother would begin embroidering clothes for him or her and would continue to do so until the child married.

Funeral Costume

In matters of death, Eastern European costume was similar to Southern European costume. Women in particular would don black clothing and embark on a period of mourning, which could last a few weeks or a few years, depending on the closeness of the relative and the traditions of the community. A rather macabre ceremony in Hungary involved a woman who had lost her husband embroidering a set of sheets that would one day be used to wrap her up at her own funeral. In Romania, the carriers of a coffin would have cloths **cross-stitched** in red and black draped over their shoulders; these cloths were supposed to protect the dead person's spirit.

Glossary

Note: Specialized words relating to clothing are explained within the text, but those that appear more than once are listed below for easy reference.

Appliqué a technique of decoration in which pieces of cloth are stitched onto a background to create a picture

Balkans the group of countries that occupy Southeastern Europe; these include Greece, Yugoslavia, Albania, Romania, and Bulgaria

Bolero jacket a short jacket ending at the waist

Byzantium a Greek city founded in the seventh century B.C.; this city became the center of one of the most powerful empires in the east

Chemise a dress or dress-like garment that hangs down straight from the shoulders

Cockade a circular badge depicting national colors

Constantinople the name given to Byzantium in A.D. 330 by the Roman Emperor Constantine

Crossbow a weapon that fires an arrow-like bolt using a string held under tension and then released

Cross-stitch a type of needlework in which an image is made from pairs of stitches that cross over each other

Crusades a series of European military expeditions that took place in the 11th, 12th, and 13th centuries, aimed at recovering the Holy Land from the Muslims

Deacon a clergyman below the rank of priest (often training to be a priest)

Diaspora the name for the dispersion of the Jews from their homeland of Israel, beginning around the eigth century B.C.

Doublet a padded jacket worn by men between the 14th and 17th centuries

Embroidery the art of decorating cloth using colored stitching

Joupane a colored undergarment

Kolpak a cloth bag that hangs over the *busby* (a Russian fur hat)

Kontoush a Persian garment worn by nobles

Liturgical relating to the established form of worship within a church

Mass the Christian ceremony in which bread, representing the body of Christ, and wine, representing the blood of Christ, are consumed

Middle Ages a period of European history lasting from the fifth century A.D. to the fall of Constantinople in 1453

Mongols people originating from Mongolia

New Testament the second part of the Christian Bible concerned mainly with the life of Christ

Old Testament the first part of the Bible that begins with the creation of the earth and charts the origins and ancient history of the Jewish people

Pallium a simple draped tunic, similar to those worn by Greek philosophers

Patriarch a title given to the most senior bishops of the Orthodox and Roman Catholic churches

Pelisse on a man, a pelisse refers to the fur-lined cloak that was often worn by hussars; on a woman, it is a long cloak that reaches down to the ankles

Placket a slit or opening in a piece of clothing that covers buttons, seams, or the tops of the pockets

Roman Catholic the largest section of the Christian Church headed by the Pope

Slavs one of the largest ethnic groups in Eastern Europe and Russia

Stole a long vestment worn by a priest that hangs down to the knees; also a long scarf or shawl worn by a woman

Talmud a literary collection containing Jewish religious law

Trinity the Christian idea of God as composed of three parts: the Father, the Son, and the Holy Spirit

Timeline

A.D. 330	The Roman Emperor Constantine renames Byzantium "Constantinople" and founds the Byzantine Empire.
370	Invaders from Asia invade and ravage much of Eastern Europe.
5th century	Germanic tribes take over most of Central and Eastern Europe.
870	The Eastern Orthodox religion begins to spread throughout Eastern Europe; ecclesiastical dress begins to follow the Byzantine style.
988	Eastern Orthodox religion is introduced into Russia.
1096–1272	Pope Urban II begins a war, known as the Crusades, to snatch the Holy Land from the Muslims; this brings Western European-style costumes to Eastern European countries.
1218–1405	Mongol invaders from East Asia conquer Russia and several Eastern European territories; Oriental items of clothing, such as the *caftan,* appear in Eastern European costume.
1345	Ottoman Turks invade Southern Europe, leaving an Islamic influence on the clothing of the Balkans and Armenia.
1453	The Byzantine empire collapses under a Turkish invasion.
1721	Peter the Great becomes emperor of Russia and introduces Western culture into Russian society.
1812–1813	Napoleon Bonaparte, the conquering French emperor, leads his army into Russia, but his troops are defeated.
1821–1828	Greece fights a war of independence against the Ottoman Turks.
1912–1913	The Balkans is convulsed by a series of wars, first against Turkey, and then against Bulgaria.
1914–1918	World War I; Eastern Europe is devastated by four years of war.
1939–1945	World War II; Jewish peoples in Eastern Europe are almost wiped out entirely by Nazi Germany.
1945–1989	Much of Eastern Europe falls under the Communist rule of the Soviet Union; the Cold War.

Online Sources

The Costumer's Manifesto
http://www.costumes.org
An extensive Web site featuring information about world costume and hundreds of links to other good sites.

Early Renaissance Fashion Terms
http://www.furman.edu/~kgossman/history/earlyren/terms.htm
Part of the "Brief History of Fashion" site, these excellent pages give clear, concise definitions of Renaissance fashion terms. Images, links, and a timeline provide additional clarification.

The Costume Page
http://members.aol.com/nebula5/tcpinfo3.html
An excellent Web site for research on ethnic or folk clothing.

The Costume Site
http://www.milieux.com/costume/
Sources for historical, science fiction, and fantasy costumers.

Britannica Encyclopedia online
http://www.britannica.com
A search under "dress" provides extensive information on the development of world clothing, including religious dress.

Further Reading

Elliot, D. *Europe's History*. Hove, England: Wayland, 1994.

Harrold, Robert. and Phyllidia Legg. *Folk Costumes of the World*. London: Cassell Academic, 1999.

Kennett, Frances. *Ethnic Dress*. New York: Checkmark Books, 1995

Peacock, John. *Costume: 1066–1990s*. London: Thames and Hudson, 1986.

Schick, I.T. *Battledress: The Uniforms of the World's Great Armies, 1700–Present*. London: Artus, 1993.

Synge, Lanto. *Art of Embroidery : History of Style and Technique*. England: Woodbridge, 2001.

Stibbert, Frederick. *European Civil and Military Clothing: From the First to the Eighteenth Century* (Dover Pictorial Archive Series). New York: Dover Publications, 2001.

About the Author

Dr. Chris McNab is a writer and editor who specializes in cultural and military history. After completing a degree in Classical culture and a Ph.D. in theology and literature, Chris went on to lecture in U.S./European literature and history at the University of Wales before establishing himself as a full-time writer. His publications on the theme of costume include *Modern Military Uniforms* and *Twentieth-Century Uniforms*, while recent historical work includes essays on ancient Egyptian civilization for *The Literature of Travel and Exploration*, and editorial contributions to *Twentieth-Century Jewish Writers* and *The Encyclopedia of Censorship*. It is in the field of military history in particular that Chris has published most widely, authoring over 13 books on topics ranging from the Vietnam War to histories of small arms. Chris lives in south Wales, U.K.

Index